Amazing Animals
Seals

Please visit our Web site, www.garethstevens.com. For a free color catalog of all our high-quality books, call toll free 1-800-542-2595 or fax 1-877-542-2596.

Library of Congress Cataloging-in-Publication Data

Wilsdon, Christina.
  Seals / Christina Wilsdon.
     p. cm. — (Amazing animals)
  Includes index.
  ISBN 978-1-4339-4026-2 (pbk.)
  ISBN 978-1-4339-4027-9 (6 pack)
  ISBN 978-1-4339-4025-5 (library binding)
  1. Seals (Animals)—Juvenile literature. I. Title.
  QL737.P64W57 2011
  599.79—dc22
                                                2010016539

This edition first published in 2011 by
Gareth Stevens Publishing
111 East 14th Street, Suite 349
New York, NY 10003

This edition copyright © 2011 Gareth Stevens Publishing.
Original edition copyright © 2006 by Readers' Digest Young Families.

Editor: Greg Roza
Designer: Christopher Logan

Photo credits: Cover, back cover, pp. 16–17, 17 (bottom left and right), 18 (bottom), 20–21, 21 (bottom), 34–35, 36–37, 37 (bottom), 38–39, 42–43, 44–45, 46 Shutterstock.com; pp. 1, 3 © Dreamstime.com/Darryl Brooks; pp. 4–5 © Dreamstime.com/Chris Johnson; pp. 6–7, 30–31 © Dynamic Graphics; pp. 8–9 © Comstock; pp. 9 (bottom), 12–13 © Photos.com; p. 10 (bottom) © Call of the Wild; pp. 10–11 © Corbis; pp. 14–15, 18–19, 32–33, 40–41 Photodisc/Getty Images; pp. 22–23 © Dreamstime.com/Wayne Johnson; pp. 24–25 © Image 100 Ltd.; pp. 26–27 © Jupiter Images; pp. 28–29, 29 (bottom) © Dreamstime.com/Eyal Nahmias; p. 41 (bottom) © Digital Vision.

Printed in the United States of America

CPSIA compliance information: Batch #CS10GS: For further information contact Gareth Stevens, New York, New York at 1-800-542-2595.

Amazing Animals
Seals

By Christina Wilsdon

Gareth Stevens
Publishing

Contents

Chapter 1
A Seal Story....................................7

Chapter 2
The Body of a Seal.........................15

Chapter 3
Kinds of Seals...............................23

Chapter 4
Seal Life.......................................31

Chapter 5
Seals in the World.........................39

Glossary.......................................44

Show What You Know.....................46

For More Information.......................47

Index..48

Chapter 1
A Seal Story

Pup Tent

The ringed seal of the Arctic is the only
seal that builds a den for its pups. The
female dives into the water under the
ice. She digs up through ice and snow to
carve out a cave. She gives birth inside
this den, and the pup stays inside it for a
few weeks.

Baby Seal rolled on the snow and ice. He sniffed, hoping to catch a scent of Mama Seal. No luck! Mama Seal was still in the water. Baby Seal felt his tummy rumble. He began to yelp and cry. Maybe if Mama Seal heard him, she would hurry back to shore!

Baby Seal's cries mixed with the yelps and whimpers of the other baby seals lying on the ice. But Mama Seal knew the special sound of her baby's voice. She could hear it clearly despite all the noise. Mama Seal swam to the edge of the ice and climbed out of the sea.

Baby Seal and Mama Seal touched noses. Mama Seal flopped onto her side so Baby Seal could drink her milk. When he was done, he was ready for a nap. Baby Seal spent most of his time lying in the sun. His fur held in the sun's warmth. Baby Seal was wrapped in his own built-in blanket!

Changing Colors

A newborn harp seal pup has yellow fur and is called a yellowcoat. The yellow turns to white after a few days, and the pup is called a whitecoat. In a few weeks, the white fur starts falling out and is replaced by the silvery coat of an adult seal.

Baby Seal weighed about 20 pounds (9 kg) when he was born. He was thin for a baby seal! Mama Seal's milk was rich in all the **nutrients** he needed for growing. Baby Seal quickly grew plump and round. Soon, he had a thick layer of fat under his skin that kept him warm, just as his fur did.

Mama Seal's body was wrapped in fat and fur, too. But she lost weight as her baby grew. She couldn't swim far away to fish while Baby Seal was so young and helpless. Sometimes she went hungry so she could stay close to him.

One day, while Mama Seal was in the water, Baby Seal saw a huge animal wander across the ice. Baby Seal had never seen a polar bear before, but he sensed danger. He curled up and pulled his head close to his body. Then he lay still as a stone. His white coat helped him look like a lump of snow. Luckily for Baby Seal, the bear wasn't hungry. It walked right by him.

Got Milk?

Seal moms make very rich milk for their young. It has 10 times more fat than cow's milk! The rich milk helps the baby grow quickly. A baby harp seal gains 3 to 5 pounds (1.4 to 2.3 kg) in 1 day!

Bad Hair Day!

While a young harp seal's adult fur is growing in, its coat looks very messy. Clumps of white fur poke out between patches of the new silver fur. That's why a young harp seal is called a ragged-jacket.

Learning to Swim

A harp seal pup that's big enough to swim is called a beater. It gets this name from the way it tries to swim by beating the water with its flippers.

By the time he was 2 weeks old, Baby Seal weighed 70 pounds (32 kg). He looked like a big, fuzzy, white sausage! But Mama Seal had grown thinner. She hadn't eaten much since Baby Seal's birth and had lost almost 40 pounds (18 kg).

Mama Seal knew that Baby Seal was old enough to survive without her. One day, she slipped silently into the ocean and swam away. Baby Seal waited many hours for her return. He and other pups on the ice yelped and cried, but it was no use. The mother seals weren't coming back.

At first, Baby Seal was able to live off the thick layer of fat he grew while drinking his mother's milk. One day, he wandered down to the water. He found that it was full of tiny shrimplike creatures. He eagerly slurped up a mouthful of them.

Baby Seal's life had changed, and soon it would change even more. He would lose his white fur and grow a new silvery coat dotted with dark spots. By the time he was 4 weeks old, he would join a herd of harp seals at home in the cold ocean.

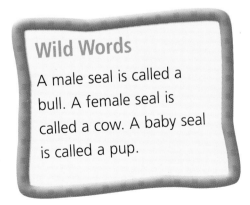

Wild Words

A male seal is called a bull. A female seal is called a cow. A baby seal is called a pup.

Chapter 2
The Body of a Seal

An eared seal, like this California sea lion, can walk and even run on land. It turns its hind flippers forward and raises itself up on its front flippers to move forward—or even backward!

At Sea and on Land

A seal is a **marine** mammal. Its body is smooth and long. Its flippers can fold up close to its body. This **streamlined** shape helps seals swim quickly and easily through ocean waters. But unlike dolphins and whales, most seals must come ashore to mate, give birth, and **molt** their fur.

Two Groups of Seals

Seals are divided into two main groups: eared seals and true seals. Eared seals have little ear flaps on the sides of their heads. Sea lions and fur seals are eared seals. All other seals are true seals. True seals have small ear openings instead of ear flaps.

When a true seal moves on land, it looks much like a giant inch worm. True seals use their front flippers to drag themselves along the ice while bending and straightening their bodies. Eared seals, however, can walk on their flippers!

true seal

eared seal

Underwater Athletes

Seals are **awkward** on land, but they're graceful and fast underwater. A seal's body bends and twists easily as it swims. A sea lion can zip along at speeds up to 25 miles (40 km) per hour for short distances.

Usually, seals find food close to the water's surface. Most can dive about 600 feet (183 m) deep and stay underwater for up to 20 minutes. Some kinds of seals can dive deeper and stay under even longer. One champion diver, the northern elephant seal, can dive nearly 1 mile (1.6 km) deep and stay underwater for up to 2 hours!

A seal can go a long time without breathing because its blood holds more oxygen than a person's blood. It also has more blood for its size than other mammals do.

Flip Up, Cool Down

A seal is so well protected against cold temperatures that it sometimes gets hot. A hot seal will hold a wet flipper in the air so that the breeze can carry away extra body heat and cool off the seal.

Different Strokes

A true seal swims by paddling with its hind flippers and swinging the back end of its body from side to side. An eared seal paddles with its front flippers. It moves them back and forth in long, powerful strokes.

Seals use their whiskers to **nuzzle** and greet one another.

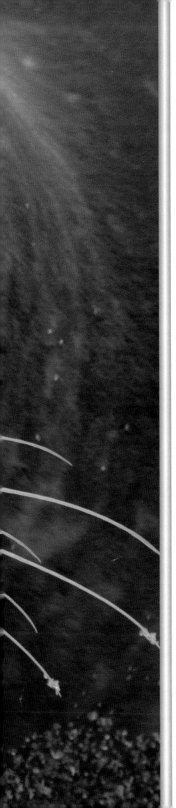

Seal Senses

On land, seals don't hear as well as people do. However, their hearing underwater is better than ours. Their excellent underwater hearing helps them find food and other seals. Many kinds of seals make sounds underwater during their **breeding** season. The sounds may be songs of males looking for mates. Scientists are now studying seals to learn if they also use sound to hunt and find their way in the dark, just as dolphins and bats do.

A seal's big eyes see well both on land and in dim, murky water. The pupils in their eyes open very wide to let in every bit of light, just like a cat's eyes do. A seal has a very good sense of smell on land, but its nostrils close up when it's underwater.

Wow-ee Whiskers

A seal's long whiskers are very sensitive. A scientist found that just one whisker from a ringed seal contains 10 times as many nerves as a whisker from a land animal! The whiskers pick up vibrations made by fish in the water.

Chapter 3
Kinds of Seals

Sea lions are seals. They get their name from the very thick fur around the necks of males. The thick fur reminded people of lions' manes. The seals shown here are Steller sea lions.

Eared Seals

All seals have ears, but eared seals have small, visible flaps on the sides of their heads. There are 14 kinds of eared seals. They live in many cold areas of the world, but not in the coldest parts of the Arctic and Antarctic as many other seals do. Sea lions and fur seals are eared seals.

Sea lions are very playful. They chase after each other in the water, ride to shore on breaking waves, and play catch with fish. Young ones play a game that looks like leap frog. Female California sea lions are the trained seals that perform in zoos and aquariums.

A sea lion pup stays with its mother for a year—longer than other seal pups do. It also goes into the water with its mother as it learns to swim. The mom lets her pup rest on her back.

Fur seals have longer snouts than sea lions, and their coats are thicker and furrier. They have long hairs like all seals plus a thick mat of short hairs called underfur. A fur seal pup isn't born with underfur. It can't go into the ocean because water soaks through the hair to the pup's skin. When it's 1 month old, a pup molts its baby hair and grows a new coat of underfur and long hairs. This new waterproof coat helps keep the seal warm while it swims.

Harp Seals

Harp seals are true seals that live in parts of the Arctic and the northern Atlantic Ocean. They eat fish, shrimp, and **krill**. Harp seal **predators** include **orcas**, polar bears, and sharks. Each year, harp seals migrate long distances between their feeding grounds and breeding grounds. In summer, harp seals hunt far up north. They start migrating south in early fall.

By late winter, the seals have reached their breeding grounds. The females give birth on wide fields of floating ice called pack ice. The males spend most of their time in the water looking for females.

A few weeks later, the females leave their pups. They band together with other harp seals to molt their fur and grow new coats. Then they head back to northern waters to feed.

Feather Feet

True seals, eared seals, and walruses belong to a group of mammals called **pinnipeds** (PY-nuh-pehdz). *Pinniped* is a Latin word meaning "wing-footed," "feather-footed," or "fin-footed." It describes the winglike feet of these animals.

True Seals

There are 19 kinds of true seals—those with ear holes in the sides of their heads and no flaps. Many true seals live in frigid Arctic and Antarctic waters and on snow-covered shores.

Each year, harp seals journey around 6,000 miles (9,655 km) between their feeding place and their breeding grounds. This is almost as long as a coast-to-coast trip across the United States and back!

A Huge Nose!
Elephant seals are named for the male's big nose, which reminds people of an elephant's trunk.

A male elephant seal can make his nose bigger by inflating it like a balloon. The biggest noses make the loudest roars, which are the best warning signs to other bulls.

Elephant Seals

Elephant seals are the biggest seals. They're true seals. Male elephant seals usually weigh between 3,000 and 5,000 pounds (1,360 and 2,270 kg), but they can weigh up to 8,000 pounds (3,630 kg)! Female elephant seals are much smaller. An average bull weighs as much as four or five females.

Elephant seals eat fish and squid. During breeding season, a thousand or more elephant seals crawl onto a stretch of beach and lie next to one another. Male elephant seals claim their territories on shore before the females arrive to give birth. They will mate with the females sometime later. These pups will be born the next breeding season.

Male elephant seals defend their territory against other bulls. When bulls fight, they belly up to each other and rear back. Then they lunge at each other with wide-open mouths, slashing with their teeth.

Chapter 4
Seal Life

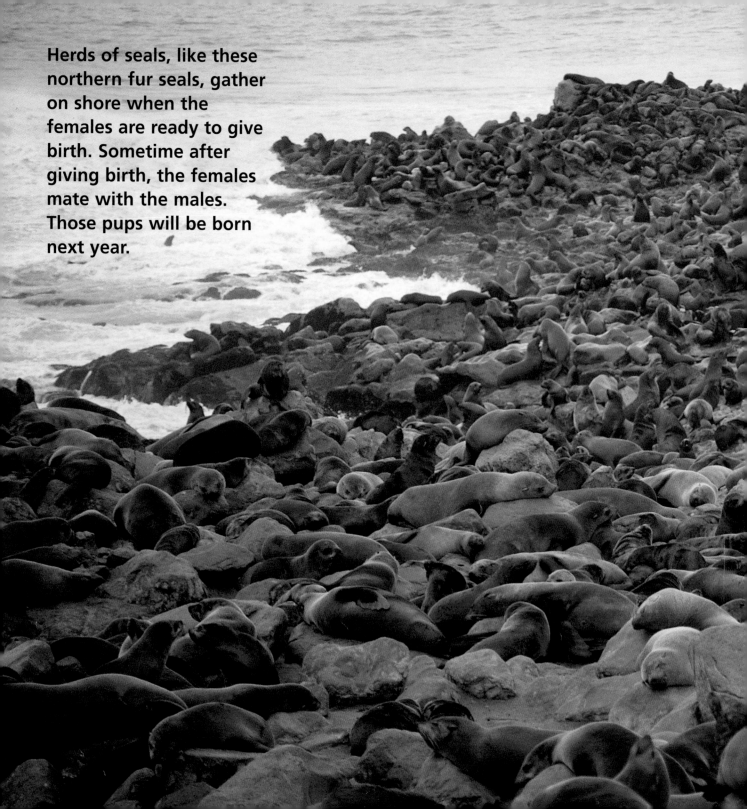

Herds of seals, like these northern fur seals, gather on shore when the females are ready to give birth. Sometime after giving birth, the females mate with the males. Those pups will be born next year.

Herds of Seals

Seals live in herds. A seal herd is a very big group of seals that feed, travel, and breed in the same place. Swimming with a group helps seals find food and protects them from predators such as killer whales and sharks. Being with other seals means there are more eyes and ears on alert for both food and danger.

Huge herds of seals, often thousands of them, gather together on shore or on floating sea ice when it's time for the females to give birth and then mate. This gathering place is called a **rookery**. Some seals swim thousands of miles to the very same sandy or rocky beach year after year. A rookery of sea lions, fur seals, or elephant seals is a very noisy place, filled with barking and roaring. But most true seals are fairly quiet on land.

How long the mom and young seal stay together depends on what kind of seal they are. A harp seal pup stays with its mom for less than 2 weeks, but a California sea lion pup stays for a year or more.

Sea Meals

Most kinds of seals eat fish to survive. But seals also eat other underwater animals, such as squid, octopuses, crabs, clams, shrimp, and other mammals. Sometimes seals will eat a bird if they can catch one.

Seals don't chew their food. They swallow it whole. If the food is too big to swallow in one gulp, the seal shakes it roughly to break it into smaller pieces. If the food has a shell, the seal uses flat teeth in the back of its mouth to crush it before swallowing.

Awesome Appetites

A seal needs lots of food to fuel its large body and survive in cold water. A female northern fur seal may eat 5 pounds (2.3 kg) of fish each day. A big elephant seal may put away 60 pounds (27 kg) of fish each day—about as much food as 240 hamburgers! A walrus can gulp down 100 pounds (45 kg) of food a day. It can eat 6,000 clams in one big meal.

Seals have sharp teeth that are good for grabbing and holding on to slippery prey.

Big Blubber!

All seals have a layer of fat called blubber. The blubber is 3 to 5 inches (7.6 to 12.7 cm) thick. Blubber helps seals stay afloat and keeps them warm in freezing waters.

Most people see seals in the wild when these sea creatures come ashore. Coming ashore is known as hauling out. Dozing in daylight lets seals bask in the sun's warmth.

Sleeping Seals

Many kinds of seals sleep in the daytime because they eat at night, when their prey swims closer to the water's surface. Seals sleep on land, but they can also sleep in water. In order to breathe, a seal sleeping in water may keep its head or even just its nose poking out of the water. Another breathing method is to bob up to the surface every 20 minutes to get a breath of air.

Old Fur, New Fur

Seals shed their fur and grow new fur once a year—in summer or fall. Molting usually takes a few weeks, but it can take a few months. For most seals, fur falls out hair by hair, just like the fur of a dog or cat when it sheds. A few kinds of seals lose large patches of fur. Some shed the whole top layer of skin with the fur attached.

Molting seals spend more time on shore. They get cold more easily in water without all their fur. As a result, they eat less even though they need a lot of energy to grow new hair. It's no wonder seals want to sleep so much!

Chapter 5
Seals in the World

Scientists are studying how global warming may affect seals, like this harp seal pup, and their polar **habitat**. If polar ice melts away, harp seal moms will have trouble finding a place to give birth.

Seals and People

People have hunted seals for thousands of years. In the Arctic, seals provided native people with everything from food to clothing. Sealskin was both warm and waterproof, and was made into coats and boots. Skins were also used to make boats called kayaks. Seal blubber was burned for light and warmth. Seal bones were carved into hooks, knives, and other tools. Native people living at the tip of South America used sealskins for sails and canoes.

Since there were only small numbers of native people who hunted seals, their hunting didn't harm the total number of seals in the world. However, about 300 years ago, hunters from other places realized people would pay a lot of money for sealskins and blubber. They traveled to where seals lived and killed millions of them. Some kinds of seals nearly became **extinct**.

The Seal's Cousin

The walrus is the only pinniped with long tusks. A walrus chops holes in ice with its tusks to reach food. It sinks the tusks into the ice to help pull itself out of the water. Male walruses show their big tusks to threaten other males.

Protecting Seals

By the early 1900s, nations realized they had to protect seals from extinction. They began to pass laws to control seal hunting. Most laws limit the number of seals that can be killed by both seal hunters and native people. Many **species** of seals, such as the northern elephant seal, have now recovered from the heavy hunting of the past. Scientists think there are more northern elephant seals today than in ancient times!

A few seals are rare, such as the Hawaiian monk seal. There are fewer than 1,200 Hawaiian monk seals left. This seal has been protected by law since 1976.

Fast Facts About Harp Seals

Scientific name	*Phoca groenlandica*
Class	Mammalia
Order	Carnivora
Size	Up to 8 feet (2.4 m) long
Weight	Up to 400 pounds (180 kg)
Life span	Up to 30 years
Habitat	Pack ice in the ocean

Many people are working to help protect seals and their habitats. Keeping our oceans clean and taking care of ocean wildlife are good for both seals and people.

Glossary

awkward—lacking agility or skill

breeding—mating and giving birth

extinct—no longer existing

habitat—the natural environment
where an animal or plant lives

krill—tiny marine creatures that look
like shrimp

marine—having to do with the sea

molt—shed old fur while new fur
grows in

nutrient—something needed for
growth and health

nuzzle—to rub something gently with
the nose or face

orca—a black-and-white whale with sharp teeth; also called a killer whale

pinniped—a true seal, eared seal, or walrus

predator—an animal that hunts other animals to survive

rookery—a place where seals come ashore in large numbers to give birth and breed

species—a category of living things that are the same kind

streamlined—shaped to make it easier to move through water or air

Seals: Show What You Know

How much have you learned about seals? Grab a piece of paper and a pencil and write your answers down.

1. Why is a newborn harp seal called a yellowcoat?

2. For what reasons do seals come ashore?

3. What are the two main types of seals?

4. Which type of seal can dive the deepest and stay underwater the longest?

5. Which seal sense is better underwater than it is on land?

6. What does *pinniped* mean?

7. What is the largest type of seal?

8. About how much food does an elephant seal eat every day?

9. What is blubber?

10. About how many Hawaiian monk seals are left?

1. Because its fur is yellow. 2. To mate, give birth, and molt their fur. 3. Eared seals and true seals 4. The northern elephant seal 5. Hearing 6. Wing-footed, feather-footed, or fin-footed 7. The elephant seal 8. 60 pounds (27 kg) of fish 9. A thick layer of fat that keeps a seal warm in cold temperatures. 10. Fewer than 1,200

For More Information

Books

Becker, John. *The Northern Elephant Seal*. Detroit, MI: KidHaven Press, 2005.

Leon, Vicky. *A Colony of Seals: The Captivating Life of a Deep Sea Diver*. Montrose, CA: London Town Press, 2005.

Markle, Sandra. *Leopard Seals*. Minneapolis, MN: Lerner Publications, 2009.

Web Sites

Friends of the Elephant Seal
www.elephantseal.org
Find out everything there is to know about elephant seals and other marine mammals.

Seals
www.antarcticconnection.com/antarctic/wildlife/seals
Read interesting facts about six different types of seals.

Publisher's note to educators and parents: Our editors have carefully reviewed these Web sites to ensure that they are suitable for students. Many Web sites change frequently, however, and we cannot guarantee that a site's future contents will continue to meet our high standards of quality and educational value. Be advised that students should be closely supervised whenever they access the Internet.

Index

A

Antarctic 25, 27
Arctic 8, 25, 26, 27, 41
Atlantic Ocean 26

B

beater 12
birth 8, 13, 17, 26, 29, 32,
　33, 40
blubber 35, 41
breeding 21, 29, 33
breeding grounds 26, 27

E

eared seals 16, 17, 19, 25, 26
ear flaps 17, 25
elephant seals 18, 28, 29, 33,
　34, 42
extinct 41, 42
eyes 21

F

fat 10, 13, 35
feeding grounds 26, 27
females 8, 13, 25, 26, 29, 32,
　33, 34
fish 10, 21, 25, 26, 29, 34
flippers 12, 16, 17, 18, 19
food 18, 21, 33, 34, 41
fur 9, 10, 11, 13, 17, 24, 26, 37
fur seals 17, 25, 32, 33, 34

H

habitats 40, 42, 43
harp seals 9, 10, 11, 12, 13, 26,
　27, 33, 40, 42
Hawaiian monk seal 42
hearing 21
herds 13, 32, 33
hunting 21, 41, 42

M

males 13, 21, 24, 26, 28, 29,
　32, 41
mate 17, 21, 29, 32, 33
migrate 26
milk 9, 10, 13
molt 17, 25, 26, 37

P

pinnipeds 26, 41
predators 26, 33
pups 8, 9, 12, 13, 25, 26, 29,
　32, 33, 40

R

ragged-jacket 11
ringed seal 8, 21
rookery 33

S

sea lions 16, 17, 18, 24, 25, 33
sealskins 41
sense of smell 21
South America 41
swimming 9, 10, 12, 13, 17,
　18, 19, 25, 33

T

territory 29
true seals 17, 19, 26, 27, 29, 33

W

walruses 26, 34, 41
whiskers 20, 21
whitecoat 9

Y

yellowcoat 9